MW00890034

The Let Them Approach

A Transformative Concept Everyone's
Talking About

Melinda Bennett

Disclaimer

This book is an unofficial biography of [Melinda Bennett]. It is based on publicly available information and the author's research. The content is not authorized or endorsed by [Melinda Bennett] or their representatives. All opinions and interpretations are those of the author and may not reflect the views of the subject or any associated parties.

TABLE OF CONTENTS

WHY THIS BOOK?

In a culture dominated by expectations, stress, and control, the Let Them Theory is a radical departure. By emphasising "letting them," this book provides a path to inner serenity, self-liberation, and authentic living. If you've ever felt exhausted from trying to change things, angered by others, or burdened by opposing views, this book is for you. It makes you rethink your relationships, your limitations, and most importantly, how much energy you spend managing the unpredictable.

Not disregarding or withdrawing from others, but freeing oneself from unnecessary expectations. Common sense principles may be used for professional growth, interpersonal connections, and emotional fortitude. Allowing others to believe, behave, and live as they like gives you control over your life in ways you never imagined. You'll find acceptance is a strength. This book does not need you to change people. Instead, it encourages you to focus within, develop self-awareness, and adopt a peaceful mindset. You will find delight, significance, and clarity in locations where doubt and aggravation previously predominated once you embrace the freedom of "letting them."

The Let Them Theory is more than just a concept; it's a way of life and a philosophy that will affect your view on the world and the way you interact with people.

Anyone who is locked in a vicious cycle of disappointment, stressed out, or overwhelmed by conflict will find enormous relevance in this book. It's time to start living life on your terms and to cease fighting conflicts that aren't yours. The key to your peace lies within you, and this book will show you how to exploit it. Are you prepared to let go and flourish? This is where the journey to emotional release, stronger relationships, and a happier life begins.

INTRODUCTION: OVERVIEW OF THE LET THEM THEORY

Even the most unexpected moments in life may teach us vital lessons. For many years, I thought that I needed to manage other people's conduct, attitudes, and responses in order to preserve control over my life. I frequently thought it was my obligation to make sure everything went as planned, whether in friendships, relationships, or the business. I felt that I could create calm and joy if I could lead people, influence debates, or have an effect on decisions. But rather than calm, I was left feeling worn out, annoyed, and let down all the time. Things seemed to break apart more and more the more I battled to grasp on.

A simple notion came to me one day after an argument that had grown out of hand: "What if I just let them?"

What if I let them conduct as they liked, think as they pleased, and make their own conclusions free from my influence? The thought appeared radical at first. Since I had always thought that my role was to lead, correct, or fix problems, how could I take a step back? However, something wonderful happened the second I let go of my craving for control. For the first time in years, I felt lighter, more at peace, and more free.

For the first time, I learned that loving people and putting your own needs first gives true tranquility rather than attempting to change others. This simple but profound understanding gave birth to the Let Them Theory: let them. Allow them to voice their ideas. Give them the freedom to choose. Give them the freedom to live. You may relieve yourself from the weight of control and make room for pleasure, sincerity, and self-discovery by embracing people for who they are. This book will lead you through the Let Them Theory's tenets and illustrate how they may enhance your relationships, reinforce your mental health, and allow you the freedom to live a life that is actually yours.

This vacation will empower you with the tools to let go, embrace freedom, and grow, regardless of whether you're feeling overwhelmed by conflict, burdened by expectations, or simply yearning for serenity.

How I Discovered the Value of Letting Go

For the most of my life, I thought that control was a prerequisite for contentment, pleasure, and success. I reasoned that I could design the ideal existence if I could control every circumstance, every dialogue, and every result.

I was so certain that my approach was the best that I painstakingly planned, prepared, and even attempted to influence the actions of others.

However, something was always lacking in spite of my best attempts. I was disheartened by the tension in relationships when my attempts to manage things went undiscovered or unappreciated, frustrated by the chaos I couldn't control, and fatigued by the mental strain of striving to direct everything.

I discovered a surprising realization one day while reflecting: no matter how hard I tried, I couldn't control other people. I was powerless to modify their beliefs, convictions, or responses to the outer world. I was becoming exhausted and doing more damage than good when I tried to do so. I felt more disconnected from the world around me the more I held on to control. The concept of "letting go" first hit me at that point—not as a theoretical theory, but as a powerful, life-changing strategy. Letting go was about letting go of my need to control people and outcomes, not about giving up.

It had to do with letting individuals be themselves, even if that meant they didn't fit my template.

It was about embracing the circumstance as it is without attempting to alter it. I started to adopt this idea gradually, and every step I took transformed my life. I started to renounce the concept that there was only one road.

I gave up trying to control every little thing and let people grow, learn, and make errors on their own. The outcomes were very outstanding.

The formerly heated connections become more genuine and tranquil. I experienced an inner calmness I had never experienced before, combined with less anxiety and more joy. I realized that taking a step back provided me better control over my life, especially over my emotions, thoughts, and mental calm. I discovered freedom in letting go. This discovery impacted my life in unanticipated ways, and I now want to transmit this newfound wisdom to you.

The Moment I Recognized That Control Does Not Equate to Freedom

---

At one time in my life, I felt that the finest form of freedom was control. I felt that I would achieve satisfaction and tranquility if I could manage every scenario, every relationship, and every part of my day.

I was so consumed with arranging, planning, and overseeing every little thing that I disregarded the simple but strong reality: control was holding me back. It was simply another average hectic day. From morning meetings to evening workouts, I had scheduled every minute of my day to be as productive and lucrative as possible.

My phone was ringing incessantly with messages from friends, family, and colleagues who all wanted something from me. There seemed to be a continual sensation of rush and a building tension in my chest as I raced from assignment to duty. The more I fought to preserve order, the more overwhelmed I grew.

It dawned on me then. I was worn out, worried, and removed from the here and now despite my best efforts and every attempt to control the circumstance. In truth, the very control I imagined would bring me freedom was having the opposite effect.

My mind was racing all the time, and I was glued to my objectives and plans, hesitant to let go of the notion that everything would collapse if I didn't retain control. I instantly understood that being free didn't entail having total control over one's life. Letting go of the temptation to control every consequence and the pressure to execute everything correctly is the way to ultimate freedom. It was the realization that the more fiercely I battled to keep control, the less I was able to fully experience tranquility. I have to build my skill to let go.

This represented a sea shift. I began practicing surrender rather than hanging onto my stringent expectations. I learnt how to trust life's process and allow things unfold organically rather than attempting to shoehorn them into a preset pattern. I allowed myself to take a step back, embrace uncertainty, and recognize that freedom isn't about controlling everything but rather having trust that, once we stop trying to manage every tiny detail, life will work itself out.

I started letting go of my drive to control after that day.
It was a steady movement toward a more comfortable and calm existence rather than an abrupt transformation. The trick to attaining the freedom I had always craved was letting go.

How Embracing "Let Them" Transforms Lives

Despite its seeming simplicity, the remark "Let Them" has a huge influence. "Let Them" encourages us to adjust our attitude and take a step back in a world that is continually urging us to take control, be strong, and make things happen.

This philosophy advises us to allow individuals the freedom to be who they are, make their own decisions, and live their lives as they see fit, rather than seeking to fix every environment and individual to suit our tastes. It's about letting life unfold spontaneously and liberating ourselves from the temptation to manipulate other people and the events around us.

Adopting the "Let Them" mindset may improve lives as it develops a strong feeling of freedom for both ourselves and the persons we connect with.Above all, "Let Them" alters lives by releasing individuals of the weight of expectations. We relieve ourselves of the pressure of seeking to foresee, manage, and influence everything around us when we give up trying to impose results. Realizing that every individual has a unique journey, we let go of the temptation to write everyone's narrative. By adopting this mindset, we offer people the freedom to fail, develop, and learn without our meddling. This just suggests that we trust other people to take charge of their own experiences, not that we become meek or uninterested in them. It serves as a poignant reminder that even when it deviates from our chosen course of action, individuals can—and frequently do—know what is best for themselves.

Adopting "Let Them" also creates more authentic and meaningful interactions. We build an atmosphere of respect and trust when we give up seeking to push our will on other people.

Because they know they won't be misunderstood or restricted, individuals feel free to be who they are. They may open out more completely due to this feeling of freedom, which leads to closer connections. We open the way to more honest and profound relationships by minimizing the impulse to control. "Let Them" gives a novel viewpoint on interpersonal connections, whether they are friendships, family dynamics, or love pairings. It is founded on mutual respect, acceptance, and support.

In the end, accepting "Let Them" alters us in ways that go beyond how we relate with other people; it also culminates in personal liberty. We sense a deep sensation of tranquility when we give up on seeking to control the uncontrollable. We begin to trust life, ourselves, and other people. We generate new chances for ourselves when we let go of the temptation to control every scenario. True pleasure and fulfillment can only be discovered when we learn to embrace the unpredictability and let life flow spontaneously.

We learn to flow with the river rather than continuously struggling against it, thinking that when we stop resisting, life will have something nice in store for us.

In conclusion, embracing "Let Them" alters lives by giving us a way to personal freedom, fostering deeper relationships, and liberating us of the weight of control. Actively choosing to trust, let go, and allow life to develop in its own beautiful fashion is more essential than being passive.

This ideology influences not just our interactions with people but also how we perceive the outer world. We allow ourselves and others the freedom to be, to develop, and to live totally when we accept "Let Them." This simple mental change has the ability to profoundly and permanently impact every element of our lives.

THE FUNDAMENTAL PRINCIPLES OF THE LET THEM THEORY

The "Let Them" philosophy is based on a number of fundamental ideas that, when accepted, have the power to drastically alter our perspectives on relationships, personal development, and life in general. We may unleash the potential for peace, understanding, and genuine empowerment by letting go of the impulse to dominate and accepting the freedom to let others choose their own pathways. The "Let Them" doctrine is based on the following ideas, which provide a guide for building a more genuine, contented, and harmonious existence.

1. The Strength of Embracing

The idea of acceptance is central to the "Let Them" notion. Accepting others' right to exist and make their own decisions, whether or not we agree with them, is more important than agreeing with what all others do or believe. It's the knowledge that each person is on a different path that is influenced by their viewpoints, beliefs, and experiences.Accepting people for who they are and where they are in life allows us to let go of the impulse to judge or control them.

Acceptance enables us to stop playing the part of the rescuer or fixer and just be there for them. More emotional freedom for ourselves and people around us is made possible by this idea.

2. **Releasing the Need for Command**

Many of us have a deep-rooted urge for control. We often feel the need to guide things in a certain direction, whether it be in our personal life, employment, or relationships.

The "Let Them" philosophy, on the other hand, questions this way of thinking and exhorts us to give up the idea that we are in charge of everything. Letting go of control is accepting that we cannot control other people's behavior or results, and that's acceptable. It's really freeing. By letting go of the need to micromanage, we create room for development, education, and change for ourselves and the people we love. Giving up control just indicates that we trust others to follow their own path in their own time and way, not that we have stopped caring.

3. **Having faith in the procedure**

The idea that life unfolds as it should and that opposing or pushing results only leads to friction is the foundation of trusting the process philosophy.

When we accept "Let Them," we have faith that everything will work itself out in due time. This implies we trust life's inherent rhythms and allow people the freedom to navigate their own experiences, not that we passively sit back and wait for life to happen. Patience, which is necessary to trust the process, may be hard to develop in a society that expects instant results. But by cultivating this trust, we may learn to accept ambiguity and acknowledge that, ultimately, all experiences—positive or negative—have a purpose.

4. Observing Boundaries

One essential tenet of the "Let Them" concept is respecting other people's limits. Boundaries are rules that help define where one person's emotional and physical space starts and ends, not barriers that are intended to keep us apart from others. We respect each person's demand for autonomy and self-expression when we uphold limits. This idea is particularly crucial in partnerships because it fosters positive dynamics where both people feel listened, respected, and understood.

Respecting boundaries frees individuals from the demands of outside expectations and lets them develop at their own rate. Respect builds relationships, lessens conflict, and makes people feel comfortable being who they are.

5. Accepting Weakness

Although vulnerability is sometimes seen as a weakness, it is really a necessary part of progress in the framework of the "Let Them" approach. We make room for openness, honesty, and connection when we let ourselves and others be vulnerable. Being vulnerable is accepting the unknown and letting our imperfections be exposed without feeling the urge to conceal or defend ourselves. By accepting our vulnerability, we give up attempting to influence how other people see us and instead give ourselves permission to live life to the fullest. Knowing that other people's feelings and experiences are real, even if they don't match our preferences or expectations, we also give them the confidence to be vulnerable.

The path to more meaningful relationships and personal development is vulnerability.

6. Allowing People to Be Who They Are

Allowing others to be who they are without forcing our standards or opinions on them is one of the most significant tenets of the "Let Them" philosophy.

This idea urges us to accept others for who they are, flaws and all, without attempting to change them into someone we believe they ought to be. We promote an atmosphere of respect, trust, and freedom when we give people the freedom to be who they are.

This is freeing for ourselves as well as for the other person as we are no longer constrained by the urge to mold or alter other people. The goal is to embrace the variety that makes each person special and to celebrate uniqueness.

7. Allowing Individuals to Develop

Giving people the time and space they need to develop is another essential component of the "Let Them" attitude. Development is a personal, organic process that cannot be hurried or coerced. We run the danger of impeding someone else's development and infuriating them when we attempt to force them to grow before they are ready. We show our belief in people's capacity to adapt and evolve by taking a backseat and letting them develop at their own tempo. This idea is applicable to many facets of life, including relationships, personal growth, and work. Allowing individuals to develop promotes a feeling of empowerment and self-confidence and recognizes that growth is an internal process that cannot be controlled by others.

8. Letting Go of Expectations

The "Let Them" theory's central tenet is the relaxation of expectations. When people don't live up to our preconceived notions of how they should act or perform, expectations may lead to a great deal of tension and disappointment. We may begin to appreciate life as it is and escape the never-ending urge to control results when we let go of these expectations. By letting go of expectations, we enable ourselves and others to accept life's flaws without ceasing to care or aim for achievement. We allow ourselves to allow events to develop naturally without imposing strict conclusions on each encounter.

The "Let Them" theory's tenets provide a novel outlook on life that places an emphasis on acceptance, autonomy, and development. We may create an atmosphere where ourselves and people around us can flourish by adopting these fundamental principles: acceptance, relinquishing control, trusting the process, respecting boundaries, accepting vulnerability, allowing others to be themselves, creating room for growth, and letting go of expectations. The "Let Them" concept alters not just how we relate to other people but also how we see life in general. It inspires us to take a step back, have faith, and let go because we know that by doing so, we can build a peaceful, genuine, and joyful existence.

Knowing What "Let Them" Actually Means

At first look, the phrase "Let Them" may seem straightforward, but its actual meaning is far more complex. Fundamentally, "Let Them" is a call to let go of the drive for dominance and give people the flexibility to live their lives as they see appropriate.

It is a concept that pushes us to change the way we think and accept the notion that we have no control over the lives of others. Rather, we serve as their mentors, allies, and guides, letting them forge their own pathways, come to their own conclusions, and develop at their own speed.

We must first acknowledge that "Let Them" is not about indifference or apathy if we are to comprehend what it really implies. This does not mean that we should do nothing but watch others make bad decisions and not step in when needed.

Rather, it's about providing presence and support without attempting to control results or impose our will. It all comes down to fostering a trusting atmosphere where people are comfortable exploring their own options, making errors, and growing from them. By comprehending the core of "Let Them," we see that it is about empowering others, granting them freedom, and letting them be who they are without criticism or pressure.

It may seem contradictory to "let them" in a society that often places a higher value on control, output, and outcomes. However, it is really a deep gesture of faith. It's an understanding that each person has a unique path to follow, lessons to learn, and challenges to surmount. "Let Them" challenges us to embrace the power of acceptance and presence rather than giving in to our natural tendency to correct, control, or jump in. By doing this, we allow others to discover their own path and ourselves to see the world without as much concern about results, relieving us of needless tension and annoyance.

This idea promotes a greater feeling of empathy, comprehension, and connection, which eventually results in more contented relationships and a more tranquil existence.

Acceptance Offers Freedom

One of the most potent and freeing things we can do for ourselves and other people is to accept them.
Fundamentally, acceptance is about letting go of the need to alter, correct, or exert control over the things and people in our lives. Instead of fighting or hoping for anything else, it's about accepting things as they are.

According to the "Let Them" ideology, acceptance is respecting people for who they are, where they are, and the way they choose to live their life, not just putting up with them. This kind of acceptance offers us a freedom that changes not only ourselves but also everyone around us.

A feeling of inner calm is produced when we engage in genuine acceptance. We start to accept life as it is, flaws and all, instead of always trying to change the world to fit our ideals. We come to appreciate people's differences as a component of what makes life rich and varied, rather than condemning them for them. Acceptance frees us from the weight of expectations and the never-ending loop of annoyance that results from attempting to influence other people or uncontrollable circumstances. By doing this, we clear our minds of needless emotional stress and make room for happiness, thankfulness, and contentment.

Furthermore, acceptance encourages sincere, meaningful relationships with other people. True relationships may thrive when we accept individuals for who they are, without attempting to alter them or force our opinions on them. People open up more when they feel appreciated and understood, which makes it possible for deeper, more meaningful interactions.

Acceptance implies we recognize the intrinsic dignity of every individual, regardless of their decisions or life path.

It does not imply that we condone destructive conduct or support acts that go against our principles. With the individuals we engage with, this kind of acceptance fosters more compassion and trust.

In the end, acceptance allows us to be free from the constraints that come with attempting to criticize, control, or alter circumstances outside of our control. It also allows people to be free to be who they are. It's about accepting life in all its complexity, letting go of irrational expectations, and finding serenity in the here and now. By practicing acceptance, we give up trying to control life's flow and instead let ourselves appreciate each moment as it comes. By doing this, we find the real freedom that comes from letting go of control and accepting life as it is. A greater awareness of how everything is interrelated, a feeling of comfort, and satisfaction are all brought about by this transformational freedom.

Giving Up Control Without Going Crazy

Accepting others and oneself is one of the most powerful and freeing things we can do. At its foundation, acceptance is about letting go of the temptation to modify, correct, or control the people and things in our lives.

It's about accepting things as they are rather than battling or hoping for something other. The "Let Them" concept emphasizes that acceptance is more than just tolerating someone; it is about accepting them for who they are, where they are, and how they want to spend their life. Acceptance like this provides us a freedom that alters not just ourselves but also people around us. When we practice real acceptance, we enjoy a sense of inner serenity. Instead of always seeking to fix the world to suit our notions, we come to accept reality as it is, faults and all. Instead of condemning folks for their differences, we learn to value them as part of what makes life rich and different. The load of expectations and the never-ending cycle of dissatisfaction that results from attempting to manage other people or uncontrolled events are removed when we embrace ourselves. By doing this, we release our mind from unneeded emotional pressure and make space for joy, appreciation, and fulfillment.

Acceptance also creates true, genuine interactions with other persons. When we accept individuals for who they are, without attempting to alter them or push our views on them, meaningful friendships may grow. Deeper, more meaningful interactions are made possible when individuals feel appreciated and understood because they open up more.

Acceptance says that we recognize each person's intrinsic worth regardless of their choices or direction in life.

It does not imply that we condone behaviors that are opposed to our principles or that we accept detrimental conduct. This type of acceptance develops empathy and trust with the individuals we engage with.

Acceptance finally frees us from the limits that accompany trying to control, condemn, or modify uncontrolled circumstances. Additionally, it provides individuals the freedom to be themselves. It's about finding serenity in the present moment, letting go of unnecessary expectations, and accepting life in all its complexity.

By practicing acceptance, we stop seeking to manipulate the flow of life and instead learn to enjoy each moment as it comes. By doing this, we realize the genuine freedom that comes from accepting life as it is and abandoning control. This transforming freedom generates a sense of ease, fulfillment, and a greater awareness of how everything is interrelated. One of the toughest and most freeing things we can do on our own road is to let go of control. Many individuals assume that in order to protect ourselves, keep things steady, or accomplish our aims, control is essential.

The paradox, however, is that the more we desire to control the environment around us, the more we feel constricted, worried, and cut off from the experiences and people that actually count. The secret to obtaining satisfaction and tranquility in life is learning to cede control—not by sacrificing our ideals or identity, but by allowing ourselves the flexibility to accept life's unpredictability and trust the process. Giving up control does not entail giving up on our feeling of accountability or continuing to make beneficial adjustments in our lives. It's about having a more flexible, open attitude on life and letting go of our rigid relationship to results. We make room for progress, innovation, and surprising possibilities when we let go of the impulse to micromanage every single detail.

This does not suggest that we relinquish our objectives, goals, or moral convictions; rather, it demonstrates that we have trust in our capacity to attain them without directing every aspect of the process. It's the notion that while we are in command of our own actions and emotions, we cannot and should not strive to control every external event. We also liberate ourselves from the tension of perfectionism when we abandon control. The concept that we need to be in command of every area of our lives in order to prevent rejection or failure is often the core cause of perfectionism.

However, we run the danger of losing sight of what is really important in the drive for perfection: the beauty of imperfection, the lessons learnt from failure, and the pleasure of the journey. We allow ourselves to be human—to make errors, evolve, and learn—when we let go of the need to be faultless. Since we find our power, resilience, and authenticity in our defects, here is where we actually discover freedom. Importantly, abandoning power does not require sacrificing our identity or our core ideals. Conversely, it permits us to remain authentic while keeping responsive to life's whims. It's about retaining our moral character and sense of direction while letting life unfold naturally without attempting to shoehorn it into a predefined plan. This type of release is a great statement of self-confidence. It is the idea that we may overcome barriers and uncertainties without needing to know the answer or solution right now. We have trust that we possess the inner tenacity to change, evolve, and learn regardless of what happened. Giving up control may be especially altering in partnerships. We frequently seek to influence the actions or attitudes of others because we feel that our way is the only or best one. However, we make way for better, more authentic connections when we let go of the temptation to dominate other people. We build trust, respect, and stronger bonds when we allow individuals to be who they are without our participation or influence.

This is not about allowing people to hurt us or letting our standards be reduced; rather, it's about accepting that everyone has their own way and journey and that we cannot force others to change or live up to our expectations.

Finding balance is essentially about releasing control without losing yourself. It entails keeping your individuality while being adaptive in how you react to the surroundings. It's the awareness that we can let go of the impulse to be in command of everything while yet remaining rooted in our ideals, interests, and sense of purpose.

By recognizing life's unpredictability and the beauty that follows from letting go of things we cannot control, this balance helps us to appreciate life to the fullest. By doing this, we make place for more satisfaction, calm, and a stronger connection with both ourselves and other people.

GOING FOR PEACE IN DAILY CONVERSATIONS

It's easy to feel overburdened by the responsibilities of everyday living in our fast-paced, globally linked society.

The continual onslaught of responsibilities, from professional commitments to personal commitments and everything in between, may make us feel detached, anxious, and worn out. Finding calm in the middle of this commotion is not only feasible, but also necessary to preserve our wellbeing. Concentrating on the daily encounters we have, whether with loved ones, coworkers, or strangers, is one of the most effective strategies to develop inner calm. When handled mindfully and with an attitude of presence, these exchanges may provide chances for harmony, development, and connection.

Changing our perspective from seeing others as challenges or causes of stress to viewing them as fellow humans is essential to achieving harmony in day-to-day relationships.

Because of our own goals, anxieties, or expectations, we often approach relationships with a feeling of urgency.

This emphasis on results may lead to stress and worry, which keeps us from really and meaningfully engaging with people. Genuine, calm interactions become possible when we let go of the impulse to steer or control talks and just allow ourselves to be there. Every connection, whether it's a quick chat with the cashier, a quick giggle with a friend, or an in-depth talk with a family member, has the capacity to bring about serenity if it is treated with calmness and openness. Empathy training is a crucial component in finding calm in day-to-day encounters. Every individual we come into contact with has a unique collection of struggles, feelings, and life events that shape the way they manifest themselves. By developing empathy, we enable ourselves to see beyond our own viewpoint and really comprehend the perspectives of others. Even in circumstances that may ordinarily cause us to get irritated or frustrated, this can help us react with patience and compassion.

In addition to making people feel noticed and appreciated, we also bring about inner serenity when we choose to listen without passing judgment, provide assistance without expecting anything in return, and respond with love. The more empathy we cultivate, the more we understand that most encounters are about the common experience of being human, not about us.

Lastly, letting go of the drive for perfection is necessary to achieve serenity in daily encounters. We often hold ourselves and other people to irrational standards in the hopes of perfect conduct, communication, and results. Our feeling of calm might be disturbed when things don't go as planned because we may become angry or disappointed. But it's precisely these imperfections that make human connections so beautiful. We don't have to respond flawlessly or provide the ideal impression. We only need to be willing to connect and present ourselves with honesty and openness. We relieve ourselves of needless worry and make room for true calm when we accept life's messiness and give up attempting to control how every connection turns out.

Accepting the ebb and flow of human connection with grace and presence is the key to finding serenity in daily relationships, not avoiding confrontation or acting as if everything is ideal. It involves making the decision to react patiently, empathetically, and kindly even in the face of difficult situations. It also involves just allowing ourselves to be really present in every moment and letting go of the urge for perfection or control. By doing this, we lay the groundwork for a foundation of calm that penetrates our everyday lives, our relationships, and eventually our inner selves.

Allowing Them to Express Their Own Opinions

Giving people the freedom to express their thoughts is one of the most potent and freeing things we can do in a society where views are continuously exchanged, discussed, and sometimes contested. It's simple to get caught up in the want to refute, correct, or alter someone else's remarks, particularly when their opinions or assertions diverge from our own. However, we can promote an atmosphere of mutual respect, openness, and understanding by practicing the skill of allowing people to express themselves freely—without criticism or interference. Deeper relationships, less stress, and more meaningful discussions may result from this little but significant change.

Allowing someone to express themselves does not obligate us to support or agree with all they have to say.

It's about respecting their freedom of expression, whether or not we agree with them. In actuality, we often learn the most about the world around us by hearing other points of view. We make room for others to feel heard, appreciated, and respected when we let them express their truth without feeling compelled to add our own thoughts.

This improves our comprehension of other viewpoints and fortifies our bonds with one another, both of which eventually aid in our personal development.Allowing people to express themselves freely also promotes a genuine culture. People are more inclined to express who they really are when they feel free to talk honestly and freely without worrying about criticism or rejection. Relationships that are more honest, open, and where communication is unrestricted might result from this transparency. Because we are interacting with one another as our true selves and are not constrained by society standards or expectations, it enables us to connect on a deeper level. Allowing people to express themselves freely also gives us the gift of honesty as it makes it simpler to share our own ideas and emotions without worrying about being rejected or silenced.

Furthermore, allowing people to express their opinions helps reduce stress and avoid needless confrontation. Disagreements often occur because individuals feel ignored or misunderstood rather than because they are innately hostile or combative. We provide people the affirmation they need to feel understood when we listen to what they have to say without attempting to quickly refute or correct it.

More fruitful discussions may result from this, allowing both sides to voice their opinions and identify grounds of agreement. Allowing someone to talk freely fosters an environment of respect and understanding amongst people, even if we don't end up agreeing. This may greatly reduce needless conflict.

However, allowing people to express themselves does not include putting up with offensive or damaging words.
It's critical to understand that, even while we should support free expression, we also have an obligation to establish limits when called for. It's OK to defend ourselves or others against cruel, discriminatory, or destructive remarks and to politely address the matter. Allowing someone to express their opinions does not imply keeping quiet about injustice; rather, it refers to creating an atmosphere that values free communication while upholding decency and compassion.

In the end, allowing people to express themselves freely means appreciating the variety of human experience and realizing the worth of each individual's voice. It's about listening to people with an open mind and heart and letting them express themselves without worrying about criticism or rejection.

By doing this, we not only broaden our own perspective on the world but also foster a more genuine, courteous, and kind environment for dialogue.

The Key to Ignoring Superfluous Drama

In a world full of noise and diversions, needless drama may sometimes seem like an inevitable aspect of day-to-day existence.There are always circumstances or individuals that appear to enjoy causing confusion, conflict, and needless strain in our interpersonal relationships, at work, or in our communities. The ability to separate ourselves from needless drama, discern when it isn't worth our effort, and regain our mental clarity is the key to ignoring it. We can live more purposeful, balanced, and happy lives if we can master the tremendous art of avoiding drama.

Acknowledging needless drama for what it is is the first step towards avoiding it. Drama often arises from individuals projecting their own emotional demands, disappointments, or anxieties onto other people. It may show up as unwarranted arguments, gossip, or even passive-aggressive conduct.

We may start to emotionally and psychologically distance ourselves from this drama by realizing that it is more about the person who is causing it than it is about us. We may stop taking things personally when we realize that we have no control over the feelings or actions of others. This change in viewpoint is essential because we can no longer let other people's drama dictate our emotions or state of mind once we stop internalizing it. The ability to establish sound boundaries is another essential skill for avoiding drama. This entails being aware of when to leave discussions or circumstances that are driven by animosity or confrontation.

Establishing boundaries is about safeguarding our mental and emotional health, not about being impolite or dismissive. It's totally appropriate to gently excuse ourselves or change the subject to something more constructive if a discussion begins to wander into gossip or needless drama. Boundaries also apply to how we interact with other people; we may reduce the amount of drama in our lives by choosing to be with positive and encouraging individuals instead of those who feed off negativity. Establishing these limits serves to reaffirm that we cannot compromise our tranquility and that we are not required to engage in every circumstance that requires our attention.

Gaining emotional intelligence is another effective way to block out pointless drama. This entails developing the ability to control our own emotions and react deliberately as opposed to rashly. It's simple to become defensive or provoked in a dramatic circumstance. However, we may establish a buffer between the stimulus (the drama) and our reaction by engaging in mindfulness and emotional self-regulation exercises. This enables us to avoid being overwhelmed by the situation's emotional intensity and instead adopt a more composed, measured response. In addition to preserving our peace, we demonstrate to others that their efforts to incite conflict are powerless over us by reacting calmly and avoiding the drama.

Concentrating on what is really important to us is one of the best strategies to block out pointless drama. We are less prone to being sidetracked by the turmoil around us when we have a strong connection to our own values, objectives, and priorities. The little disputes or drama that occur in our life appear less important if we are clear about our goals and purpose. We are able to see that it is preferable to focus our time and efforts on activities that are in line with our actual aspirations rather than being mired in pointless drama or trivial arguments.

We will be less inclined to participate in or pay attention to the drama that others may attempt to create if we concentrate more on the things that make us happy, fulfilled, and progress. Ultimately, avoiding needless drama requires self-compassion exercises. It's simple to get enmeshed in other people's drama, particularly if we hold ourselves accountable or feel bad for their emotional states. But it's crucial to remember that we have no influence over other people's actions, and it's not our place to solve their issues or put up with their negativity. We strengthen the notion that we have the ability to decide where to spend our attention and energy by treating ourselves with kindness and admitting that we deserve to live in peace and tranquility. Self-compassion enables us to concentrate on taking care of ourselves and our well being rather than acting out drama.

The goal of ignoring needless drama is to establish and maintain a peaceful inner environment despite the mayhem outside. Setting clear boundaries, skillfully managing our emotions, focusing on our objectives, practicing self-compassion, and separating from other people's emotional storms are all necessary.

Adopting these techniques helps us regain our strength and vitality, which enables us to live more fulfilled, focused, and clear lives.

The key to ignoring needless drama is ultimately not to completely avoid confrontation, but rather to decide not to participate in the drama that isn't beneficial to us and to remain dedicated to our own mental health.

Giving Others the Freedom to Choose

Giving people the freedom to make their own decisions is one of the most humane and powerful things we can do for them. We often find ourselves intervening to provide counsel, make choices for others, or even nudge them in the path we think is best out of a desire to assist, safeguard, or mentor. Even while this could be done out of love or concern, it may inadvertently undermine their feeling of independence and personal development.

In addition to respecting others' uniqueness, letting them make their own decisions without our input or criticism builds mutual trust and a stronger bond.Fundamentally, recognizing and honoring others' agency means letting them make their own decisions. Regardless of whether we agree with them or believe they are the best option, each person has the right to their own beliefs, preferences, and choices.

Allowing someone to follow their own path respects their right to live life as they see fit, grow from their errors, and develop in ways that may not be consistent with our own expectations or experiences. We create an atmosphere where people can trust their intuition and themselves when we take a backseat and allow them to make their own decisions. This fosters resilience and self-assurance.

It's important to keep in mind that letting others make their own decisions does not entail doing nothing when we see them making a choice that might cause regret or injury. A delicate balance must be struck between providing direction and honoring individuality. Supporting people without forcing our will on them is crucial. The choice must ultimately be theirs, even if we express our opinions, make recommendations, or pose challenging questions. By doing this, we respect their autonomy to choose their own path while being a caring influence in their life. This strategy builds trust because people know they can count on us to help them, but they also realize that they have the freedom to make their own decisions.Relationship development also greatly benefits from letting people make their own decisions.

Allowing each individual to make their own choices promotes independence and respect for one another in all types of relationships, including friendships, romantic partnerships, and family interactions. It may stop the power battles that often occur when someone attempts to exert control or influence over another. Individuals may be seen as equal partners who respect one another's autonomy rather than as sources of approval or affirmation. This fosters a more positive dynamic in which everyone feels free to express themselves and make choices without worrying about criticism or reprisal. As a consequence, there is a stronger, more genuine bond that is resilient to life's obstacles.

Furthermore, we impart the important lesson of responsibility to others when we let them make their own decisions. Whether they result in success or failure, the decisions we make help to define who we are as people. We learn to be responsible for the results, both good and bad, when we take responsibility for our choices. We deny people the chance to develop and learn from their experiences when we continuously step in or protect them from the repercussions of their behavior.In the end, giving people the freedom to make their own decisions and deal with the fallout helps them become more capable decision makers, more responsible, and more self-aware.

It may sometimes be challenging to take a back seat and allow people make their own decisions, particularly when we firmly believe that our method is the right one. It may be difficult to fight the want to "fix" things or talk someone out of a choice we think is bad. But it's crucial to understand that letting people make their own decisions also means having faith in their ability to grow from their mistakes. Everything contributes to the process of personal development, regardless of whether the choice works out successfully or results in a lesson discovered via adversity. We help people on their path to become more independent, self-assured, and empowered people by assisting them in making their own decisions.

Giving people the freedom to choose for themselves is a sign of great love and respect.

It calls on us to let go of our urge for dominance and have faith in other people's ability to manage their own lives. We give kids room to develop, learn, and flourish in their own special ways by doing this. At the same time, we promote more genuine, healthy relationships based on autonomy, respect, and trust. In the end, having the ability to choose is a gift that gives us and others around us the ability to live lives with more self-assurance, contentment, and purpose.

CHANGING RELATIONSHIPS WITH LET THEM

The "Let Them" strategy has a transforming impact, particularly when it comes to how we interact with other people. The need to dictate, counsel, or alter the other person in any kind of relationship—romantic, family, or professional—often results in annoyance, miscommunications, and animosity. This conduct restricts progress and causes conflict rather than promoting true connection. On the other hand, adopting the "Let Them" approach provides a novel viewpoint on how we engage with others in our life. In addition to relieving ourselves of needless stress, letting people be who they are, make their own choices, and grow from their experiences also makes room for deeper, more meaningful connections.

Giving people the freedom to choose their own lives is central to the "Let Them" ideology. This entails relinquishing the urge to continuously control or guide other people's behavior in relationships.We let others take charge of their own lives rather than intervening to solve issues, make choices, or influence them toward our ideal results. Making this change may be challenging, particularly if we have strong feelings for someone and wish to keep them safe.

However, we demonstrate our respect and trust for others when we allow them the freedom to make their own decisions. This gives them more authority and inspires them to develop in their own unique manner. The change in interpersonal dynamics that "Let Them" brings about is among its most significant impacts. We adopt the position of a helpful presence—someone who listens, provides encouragement, and watches without enforcing our will—instead of seeing ourselves as problem-solvers or controllers. The other person feels more appreciated and understood as a result of this shift in strategy. They experience acceptance for who they are and what they chose to do, as opposed to criticism or condemnation. Any relationship must have a feeling of safety and openness, which is created by this acceptance. A relationship becomes stronger, more genuine, and more enduring when both partners realize they can make their own choices without worrying about criticism or coercion.

"Let Them" transformation also entails letting go of irrational expectations. We often go into relationships with preconceived ideas about how things should work out, what our loved ones or partners should do, or how they ought to act.

These demands may be restrictive, leading to needless stress and disappointment when others fail to live up to them. We let go of these expectations and let the connection develop organically when we embrace the "Let Them" mentality. This is about acknowledging that everyone has a unique journey and that everyone experiences development and change at a different pace, not about letting up on our principles or limits. We may achieve more acceptance and understanding when we stop attempting to shape the people in our life into perfect partners or copies of ourselves.

When we accept "Let Them" in our relationships, trust is another important change that takes place. Any successful relationship is built on trust, but when we feel the need to step in and control someone else's life, that trust may sometimes become strained. We show that we trust others to manage their own lives when we allow them to make their own choices, even if we don't always agree with them. By demonstrating that we value the other person's opinion and have faith in their ability to overcome obstacles, this act of trust deepens our relationship. Because they are not under continual scrutiny or pressure to live up to someone else's expectations, both partners feel comfortable being themselves in this setting of mutual trust.

Additionally, the "Let Them" mentality permits connections to foster personal development. We often overlook the fact that we ourselves need room to develop when we attempt to dominate or sway others.

Control or expectation-based relationships have the potential to strangle both people since they inhibit personal development and expression. We provide ourselves the right to make our own decisions when we allow others to do the same. As a consequence, there is a connection that honors both individual and group development, allowing everyone to grow, learn, and adapt without worrying about limitations or criticism. In this sense, "Let Them" not only changes the other person but also changes ourselves by promoting an atmosphere of respect, understanding, and growth.

The key to changing your relationships with the "Let Them" concept is to embrace trust, freedom, and autonomy. It's about realizing that we cannot—and ought not to—control other people's choices, behaviors, or lives. Rather, we need to provide acceptance, respect, and support while letting people make their own decisions.

Both parties feel appreciated, heard, and empowered in these better, more satisfying partnerships.

Relationships based on trust, freedom, and sincere connection are created when we let go of the impulse to control and accept others for who they are. Our lives might therefore become more peaceful and fulfilled as a result of these connections being stronger, deeper, and more durable.

When to Take a Backseat and Allow Them to Develop

One of the most crucial things we can learn in our interactions with other people is when to back off and give them space to develop. Sometimes, whether it's a friend, family member, or a romantic partner, our natural tendency is to step in, provide advice, or even defend individuals we love. But real development and change often occur when we give people the freedom to choose for themselves, deal with their own problems, and grow from their own errors. The secret is to know when to let go, take a step back, and have faith that they can manage their trip alone.

When the person you are worried about is refusing assistance or guidance, it's one of the first indications that it may be time to take a step back. Accepting this might be challenging, particularly if we think we know what's best for them.

However, in these situations, exerting greater pressure or giving more unsolicited counsel may cause conflict and distance. Individuals must believe they are free to choose for themselves, even if that choice differs from what we would recommend. They may need some time to work things out on their own if they are not seeking assistance or are deliberately defying your advice. Stepping back in these circumstances demonstrates your respect for their autonomy and your faith in their capacity to make the best choices for their own development.

When someone expresses a wish for independence or self-reliance, it's also crucial to take a step back. We all want greater control over our lives as we get older, and young adults and those going through major life transitions may find this especially true. It's critical to respect someone's wish to be independent when they express the need to do so. Giving children the autonomy to make their own decisions, even if it might be hard to let go, boosts their self-esteem and gives them the ability to assume accountability for their future. Giving the other person the freedom to choose their own path may help both parties build more balanced, healthy dynamics. This is particularly true in relationships when one partner has been more protective or domineering.

Giving someone space to develop is often the greatest way to help them; stepping back doesn't mean leaving them in their hour of need. A person may need time to think things out and handle them independently when they encounter difficulties in their relationships, profession, or personal growth. They may be prevented from developing their own problem-solving skills and from learning critical life lessons if you try to fix their issues for them or intervene too soon. Giving kids the chance to deal with these difficulties on their own makes them stronger and more resilient. In this situation, you may help them by believing that they can manage things independently and that confronting hardship head-on often leads to progress.

When someone's development necessitates making errors and growing from them, that's another moment to take a step back. Despite our desire to protect our loved ones from suffering, failure and errors are necessary for personal development. Allowing someone to make choices, even if they cause suffering or short-term setbacks, is sometimes the wisest course of action.

They develop resilience, acquire priceless life experience, and strengthen their ability to face obstacles in the future by trial and error. We deny children the chance to develop if we constantly intervene to stop errors or provide answers.

One of the most effective ways to demonstrate your confidence in someone's capacity to manage life's challenges is to take a step back and let them face the inevitable results of their decisions. Furthermore, when you see that your engagement is no longer beneficial and may even be impeding their advancement, it's critical to take a step back. Our desire to assist others might sometimes backfire. For instance, the other person may feel undercut or unable to handle their own affairs when we are too concerned or dominating. It's time to reevaluate your position and take a step back when you start to see that your presence is limiting their confidence or independence. In addition to empowering them, allowing them the freedom to take initiative and make their own choices instills confidence in their own skills. They are able to develop in ways that they would not have otherwise been able to because of this change in accountability.

Even if we believe the individual in issue is making a mistake, it's crucial to take a step back after they have made their aims and aspirations known. Even if we may believe we know better, we should appreciate other people's decisions since they let them choose their own path, even if they differ from our own. A choice isn't always bad for them just because it doesn't fit with our own experiences.

In these situations, taking a back seat entails acknowledging their independence and the fact that their path differs from ours. Everybody develops in their own time and manner, and sometimes the greatest course of action is to help them remotely so they may take charge of their own lives.

Finally, when we see that our emotional connection is impairing our judgment, it is critical to take a step back. Acting out of fear, worry, or a desire to exert control over the situation might be simple when we are very emotionally invested. One of the most crucial steps in learning to let go is realizing when our emotions are controlling us and keeping us from giving others the room they need to develop. By taking a step back, we offer ourselves the chance to see things more clearly and give the other person the space they need to thrive.

In conclusion, a critical ability that fosters autonomy, trust, and personal growth is understanding when to back off and allow others to flourish.
It's about realizing that every person's path is different and that by taking a step back, we provide others the opportunity to grow, learn, and acquire the resilience they will need in the future.

Even though it might be hard to let go, particularly when we have a profound affection for someone, the space we make by taking a step back often gives us the freedom to develop. In the end, we encourage others by letting them follow their own path, make their own decisions, and develop to the fullest extent possible rather than by dominating or interfering.

The Value of Sound Boundaries

The foundation of harmonious and satisfying partnerships is sound limits. They provide a clear knowledge of each person's needs, desires, and boundaries by defining where one person stops and another starts. Setting boundaries reflects self-respect and self-awareness and goes beyond simple self-defense. Relationships may become poisonous, manipulative, or exhausting when there aren't appropriate limits. It is crucial to comprehend the significance of limits in order to preserve one's physical, mental, and emotional health. They enable people to live genuinely without compromising their sense of self, cultivate respect, and encourage healthy connections.

The protection of your mental well-being is one of the main reasons boundaries are crucial. It is simple to absorb other people's feelings, demands, and expectations when boundaries are absent. Stress, exhaustion, and resentment may result from this. You can feel pressured to constantly satisfy others, say yes when you want to say no, or constantly put others' demands ahead of your own when you don't set clear boundaries.By enabling you to put your own emotional needs first without feeling guilty, healthy boundaries help you avoid this. Establishing boundaries helps you make the time and space required for emotional health, personal development, and self-care. You are more likely to get into partnerships built on respect and concern for one another when you respect your own wants and emotions.

Boundaries are essential for preserving respect in relationships as well as for emotional well-being.
Setting boundaries makes it obvious how you want other people to treat you. They provide the parameters for your interactions with others and determine your boundaries.
People are better able to comprehend your requirements and preferences when you communicate your limits in an authoritative and clear manner. This lessens the possibility of miscommunication, animosity, or uncertainty regarding appropriate conduct.

A respectful relationship dynamic where both parties respect one another's needs is made possible by healthy limits. They serve as an invitation to candid dialogue in which both parties are free to express their emotions, request what they need, and provide assistance in ways that are mutually beneficial. The time and energy protection that good limits provide is another important feature. It is simple to overextend ourselves in an effort to satisfy deadlines, satisfy responsibilities, or please others in a society where demands are made of us all the time. If you don't have limits, you may feel overburdened, overextended, and disregard your own health.

By establishing limits, you may make sure that you are not sacrificing more time, effort, or resources than you can manage. You may safeguard your personal time for relaxation, interests, and pursuits that enhance your general well-being by learning to say no when it's essential. You may maintain balance and prevent burnout by managing your time more skillfully with the support of healthy limits. Setting limits is also crucial for promoting self-reliance and self-worth. We often jeopardize our feeling of self-worth when we let people to transgress our boundaries, whether intentionally or inadvertently. It might cause us to feel helpless or in control, which lowers our confidence.

We show ourselves and others that we respect our own needs, wants, and sense of self by establishing clear boundaries. Setting boundaries gives us the ability to make choices that are consistent with our beliefs and boosts our self-confidence. As we learn to speak out for ourselves in positive, healthy ways, this feeling of empowerment boosts our self-esteem.

Additionally, establishing appropriate boundaries is crucial to fostering balance in relationships, particularly in situations where reliance is likely to develop. It's simple to get into codependent behaviors, when one person's wants are continuously put above the other's, whether in a friendship, love relationship, or professional setting.

An inappropriate degree of connection or dependence on one another, sometimes at the price of one's own wellbeing, characterizes codependent relationships. By preserving a healthy degree of dependency where both people may assist one another without losing themselves in the process, boundaries help avoid this. While maintaining a loving and supportive relationship, boundaries help guarantee that each person has the freedom to be who they really are and follow their own dreams.

The fact that borders encourage constructive dispute settlement is among their most significant features. Conflict is more likely to be resolved in a courteous and productive way in partnerships when boundaries are upheld. When boundaries are crossed, it's critical to express your feelings and what you need to do going ahead. Good boundaries provide a structure for these discussions, facilitating less emotionally charged and more fruitful interactions.

They make it possible for people to discuss problems honestly and freely without worrying about reprisals or invalidation. You create the conditions for conflict resolution that respects the needs and emotions of both parties by respectfully and consistently establishing your limits. The ability to develop and find oneself is another important advantage of having good limits.

We offer ourselves the opportunity to discover our true selves when we place boundaries on the extent to which we let other people shape our decisions and convictions.

Setting boundaries keeps us true to who we really are and prevents us from being influenced by outside forces or other people's viewpoints.

They provide us the freedom to pursue our hobbies, interests, and ideals without feeling constrained or under pressure to live up to the standards of others. As we learn to make choices that are in line with our long-term objectives and actual aspirations rather than giving in to outside pressure, this freedom promotes personal development.

Last but not least, setting and maintaining good boundaries helps people stay away from toxic and harmful situations, which promotes general wellbeing. Boundaries serve as a barrier against harmful influences in social situations, the workplace, and family dynamics. You may separate yourself from people or circumstances that are emotionally taxing, manipulative, or harmful by establishing clear boundaries. This creates a secure environment in which you may flourish, work for your objectives, and cultivate relationships founded on respect and concern for one another.

Setting boundaries serves as a protective measure, guaranteeing that you are surrounded by situations and people that enhance rather than diminish your enjoyment and personal development.

To sum up, having healthy boundaries is crucial to living a happy, balanced, and powerful life because they safeguard your mental well-being, promote mutual respect in relationships, and provide the room you need for personal development and self-expression.

Establishing boundaries enables you to safeguard your time, effort, and assets while fostering connections based on mutual respect and understanding. You may design a life that fits your needs, beliefs, and objectives by accepting the significance of sound boundaries. You can also build stronger, more meaningful relationships with other people.

Helping Without Correcting

Knowing when to provide support and when to just be there without attempting to change the situation is one of the most difficult parts of any relationship, whether it be with a friend, family member, or partner. The inclination to make things better for other people comes from a place of love, concern, and a want to ease their hardships. True support, on the other hand, is about enabling someone to overcome their own obstacles with your empathy and encouragement, not about taking charge or finding solutions for them.

One crucial ability that promotes respect, development, and emotional health in relationships is supporting without correcting. Realizing that not every issue requires a solution is the first step in providing help without solving. People often don't talk about their struggles because they want help or intervention; instead, they can be seeking empathy, approval, or just a place where they can feel comfortable. The finest support someone may get when they speak up about their difficulties is a sympathetic ear and empathy. When you carefully listen to someone without immediately offering answers, you create an atmosphere where they feel respected and heard. Being present may have a profoundly therapeutic effect since it gives the person the opportunity to independently process their feelings and get insight.

We risk inadvertently undermining the autonomy and trust of the other person when we attempt to solve a situation. If we constantly intervene and take control, the individual could start to believe that they are incapable of managing their own problems or that their judgment is being questioned. It's important to acknowledge that everyone handles problems differently, and that sometimes the greatest approach to support someone is to take a backseat and let them come up with their own answers.

One effective way to encourage someone is to have faith in their capacity to manage their own issues. Instead of suggesting that they need rescuing, it conveys faith in their fortitude and tenacity. When someone receives this kind of encouragement, they become more confident and empowered because they understand they have the abilities and resources necessary to overcome obstacles in life. It's crucial to know when to refrain from giving counsel and to keep in mind that sometimes the individual may not be prepared to hear answers.

When facing personal challenges, people go through several emotional phases. Sometimes, they may not be receptive to suggestions or may just want some time to process their feelings before coming up with answers. It's crucial to respect their emotional maturity and speed. supplying consolation, assurance, or just your presence at these times may be more beneficial than supplying answers. It's OK to accept that the individual is not yet ready for guidance and to just support them as they process their emotions. Sitting quietly with someone and giving them a hug or a nice word may often provide more solace than any remedy could. Recognizing the power of encouragement is another aspect of supporting without mending.

In the long term, it may be more successful to empower people to find their own answers rather than instructing them what to do or how to accomplish it. Pose open-ended questions like "What do you think would help you feel better?" or "What have you tried so far?" to encourage them to consider their alternatives and possibilities. Without forcing your own ideas or answers on them, these kinds of inquiries promote introspection and problem-solving. Strong tools like encouragement and affirmation may help someone become more confident in their ability to make decisions and know that they can figure out the best course of action on their own.

People may need support for circumstances when they require practical assistance in addition to emotional difficulties. However, it's crucial to maintain equilibrium even while providing aid. Asking "How can I help?" is more effective than trying to repair everything at once. The other person may take the initiative to explain what sort of help they really need by answering this open-ended inquiry. Support that is both beneficial and considerate of their autonomy is ensured when it is provided in a manner that respects their wishes and limits.

For example, if someone is overburdened with work, ask them if they need help with anything so they may focus the support wherever they see fit rather than presuming they need help with a particular activity. Supporting without correcting also entails realizing that every person's path is different. What works for one person may not work for another, and finding a solution is often a personal journey.

Even if we may have unique viewpoints and experiences to offer, it's important to fight the impulse to force them on other people. For the individual you're assisting, what may have worked for you in a comparable circumstance might not be the best course of action. It's important to acknowledge that every person processes and overcomes obstacles differently, and that's a necessary part of assisting them. A crucial component of their development is letting children solve problems on their own, even if it means making errors along the way.

The need for control in relationships may also be the source of the desire to make things better. In actuality, repairing might be motivated by fear or a desire to feel wanted, but it often provides us a feeling of strength or achievement. Others may grow and develop when we give them the freedom to follow their own path and relinquish control.

This approach might be humbling since it calls for us to have faith that they will solve problems, even if it takes some time. We build more solid, respectful relationships built on mutual trust and understanding by giving up power and providing non-intrusive assistance.

Additionally, more genuine and honest interactions result from supporting without correcting. We foster an atmosphere where vulnerability may thrive when we let people talk about their difficulties without feeling obligated to provide answers.

When people know they won't be evaluated or given answers right away, they are more willing to open up and express their actual emotions. Rather, they are greeted with compassion and understanding, which promotes stronger emotional ties. Being present for someone without trying to alter or correct their circumstances and letting them be who they are completely entails providing authentic support.

In summary, the ability to help without correcting is a critical competency that fosters personal development and improves relationships. It calls for tolerance, compassion, and the conviction that people are capable of handling their own difficulties.

We demonstrate that we are sincere supporters by encouraging others, paying attention, and creating a secure environment for them to express themselves. This enables the people we care about to overcome their own obstacles. We build stronger, more lasting relationships and give people the confidence to handle their own path when we let go of the impulse to solve and concentrate on providing unconditional support.

UNDERSTANDING YOUR FEELINGS BY LETTING THEM

An essential component of the human experience is emotion. They impact how we relate with people, how we see the world, and how we make choices. But negotiating the complicated terrain of emotions may sometimes seem too much to handle. The concept of completely accepting and "letting" our emotions flow freely may seem contradictory in a society that encourages emotional restraint and self-control. However, allowing your emotions to exist, comprehending their underlying meanings, and using them as effective instruments for self-awareness and personal development are the keys to conquering them rather than denying or dominating them.

This method, known as the "Let Them" philosophy, provides a revolutionary viewpoint on emotional control.
We learn to embrace emotions and process them with compassion, empathy, and awareness rather than fighting them or trying to get rid of them. Understanding that emotions are messages to be understood rather than adversaries to be vanquished lies at the core of emotional intelligence.

A lot of us have been socialized to think that feelings like fear, sorrow, or rage are bad or should be ignored. Therefore, we attempt to conceal them, push them down, or deny them, which often makes matters worse. We can better understand what emotions are attempting to convey to us if we allow ourselves to feel them without passing judgment. For instance, melancholy may indicate a loss or an unfulfilled desire for connection, while rage may indicate a breach of our boundaries or a need for justice. We give ourselves the opportunity to comprehend the causes and meanings of these feelings when we cease fighting them. We have the option to respond consciously rather than impulsively, making sure that our actions reflect our actual sentiments and ideals.

Emotional resilience is also encouraged by letting feelings surface without passing judgment. Emotions are dynamic; they rise and fall with little warning and go just as swiftly.

We create emotional blockages that stop our emotions from flowing naturally when we fight or repress them. This might eventually cause emotional accumulation, which makes it more difficult to handle stress, sadness, or challenging circumstances. By using the "Let Them" technique, we start to realize that feelings are fleeting and do not determine who we are.

Our job is to ride them without holding on to them or letting them rule us, as they come and go like waves. Because we no longer ignore or dread emotions, this mental change aids in the development of resilience. Rather, we see them as fleeting moments that won't overwhelm us. Because we have faith that even the strongest feelings will ultimately fade, this emotional flexibility keeps us centered when faced with difficulties.

The deep feeling of self-awareness that arises is one of the main advantages of controlling emotions by allowing them to flow. We are offered a window into our inner world when we give ourselves permission to completely feel and experience emotions. Being emotionally aware enables us to relate to our needs, values, and actual selves. We may develop a better comprehension of the factors influencing our choices, behaviors, and reactions to life by recognizing and sitting with our emotions.

For instance, it may be a sign that something has to change, that a boundary hasn't been upheld, or that we have an unconscious need for something else if we often feel annoyed in certain circumstances. Rather than responding without thinking, we might pause to consider the reasons behind our feelings, which will help us better comprehend who we are.

The first step in making deliberate, empowered choices that are in line with our true aspirations and objectives is developing self-awareness. The capacity to change unfavorable emotional patterns into chances for development is a crucial component of learning to control emotions by allowing them. When we continuously push aside unpleasant feelings, we lose the chance to grow from them. For example, fear may serve as a strong motivator by warning us of possible dangers or assisting us in avoiding them. However, we could lose out on important lessons that might result in personal development if we ignore or repress our anxiety. We may learn to deal with fear in a positive, healthy manner by allowing ourselves to feel it and investigating its causes. We may accept the fear, comprehend it, and utilize it as a tool to help us develop or make better judgments. We start to use the energy of emotions for good when we transform our relationship with them from one of avoidance to acceptance, rather than allowing them to rule us.

Furthermore, greater emotional expression and communication in our relationships are made possible by allowing emotions to flow freely. In an effort to preserve peace or prevent confrontation, many of us are socialized to suppress our emotions, especially unpleasant ones.

But this behavior often results in unresolved tension or emotional detachment. We encourage more sincere and significant interactions when we accept and express our feelings honestly. We may open out to people about our real experiences rather than concealing them behind a façade of calm. This openness makes room for empathy, comprehension, and connection.

When both people feel free to express their feelings without worrying about criticism, relationships flourish.In all kinds of relationships, expressing our feelings in a healthy, polite manner may increase closeness and build trust.

Embracing our feelings not only improves our interpersonal interactions but also increases emotional intelligence. The capacity to identify, comprehend, and control our own emotions as well as to sympathize with those of others is known as emotional intelligence. We improve our capacity to recognize what we're experiencing and why by giving ourselves permission to completely experience and process emotions. Instead of responding on impulse or letting our emotions control us, this increased emotional awareness enables us to behave intelligently in any circumstance.

Additionally, it helps us to better comprehend the feelings of others, allowing us to assist and empathize in ways that deepen our bonds. A crucial component of emotional intelligence is recognizing emotions, comprehending their effects, and employing them as a guide to go through life rather than repressing or avoiding them.

Developing emotional self-control by allowing your feelings to flow also promotes mental and physical health. Our mental and physical health may suffer significantly if we suppress our feelings. Since the body internalizes unresolved emotions, emotional repression is associated with higher levels of stress, anxiety, and even physical illnesses.

We lessen the likelihood of emotional repression by letting emotions flow freely, which also reduces stress and enhances general health.
We may find relief and release pent-up emotions when we interact with our emotions in a healthy manner, such as by writing, speaking with a trusted friend, or practicing mindfulness techniques like meditation. In addition to promoting emotional well-being, this practice improves our capacity for concentration, clear thinking, and calm inner guidance while making judgments.

To sum up, allowing your emotions to rule you is a powerful process that changes how we perceive, comprehend, and deal with our emotions. We learn to accept emotions, comprehend their meanings, and utilize them as instruments for personal development rather than resisting them or allowing them to rule us. This method encourages self-awareness, emotional fortitude, and stronger interpersonal ties. We may overcome emotional obstacles and create a more balanced, genuine existence by allowing our emotions to flow freely. In addition to being a means of achieving personal recovery, accepting the whole range of our emotions opens the door to a more conscious, compassionate, and empowered way of life.

Refusing to Take Their Behavior Personally

It may sometimes be difficult to engage with others in our day-to-day lives. When people behave in ways that are perplexing, annoying, or harmful, we start to wonder why they do it. It's simple to fall into the trap of thinking that their conduct is a direct reflection of us, that it somehow relates to us, our value, or our deeds. The understanding that our behaviors are not directly related to those of others, however, is one of the most potent lessons in emotional control and personal development.

We remove ourselves from needless emotional burdens and are able to react with more composure, clarity, and understanding when we cease taking their acts personally. In actuality, people's actions are mostly a reflection of their own circumstances, challenges, and emotional states. The individuals we contact are impacted by our history, feelings, and present situation, just as we are. It's critical to understand that when someone acts hurtfully, responds adversely, or makes a casual remark, it's probably more about them than it is about us. Their actions could be a result of their own annoyances, anxieties, or insecurities. Instead of internalizing their conduct as a personal slight, knowing this enables us to take a detached view and watch their behavior with compassion.

Taking things personally often results from an exaggerated feeling of self-importance or the conviction that we are the center of the universe. We may believe that we are the center of the world and that everything that others do has some direct bearing on us. In actuality, most individuals are too preoccupied with their own problems, feelings, and ideas to pay attention to us exclusively. We may release ourselves from the burden of needless criticism and the emotional upheaval that results from taking things personally when we acknowledge that other people's actions are impacted by their inner lives.

This change in viewpoint enables us to approach circumstances with more emotional distance, seeing the actions of others as a reflection of who they are rather than a criticism of our value. We often take other people's behavior personally because we want to be liked and accepted, which is one of the key causes. Seeking approval from others is a fundamental human need, and when their behavior deviates from our expectations, we might feel rejected or undeserving. We may, however, let go of the desire for outside approval and concentrate on developing our own sense of value after we learn to not take offense at what they do. We build a strong foundation of inner serenity by establishing our sense of self on our own values, beliefs, and deeds rather than in the acceptance of others. As a result, we may communicate with others more honestly and without worrying about criticism or rejection.

We may interact in relationships with less attachment to results and more emphasis on respect, progress, and mutual understanding when we stop taking things personally.

It's crucial to understand that individuals often behave in ways that are motivated by feelings or circumstances that are unrelated to us. Someone may be struggling personally, having a rough day at work, or feeling overburdened by the demands of life.

During these times, their internal condition may have a greater impact on their conduct than any outside influences, including how they interact with us. We make room for empathy and compassion when we decide not to take offense at their behavior. We might tackle the matter with patience and understanding rather than becoming defensive or angry. Rather than being caught up in the emotional tide of someone else's hardships, this mentality change enables us to preserve our own balance.

We may avoid the trap of presuming that the behaviors of others are evil or purposeful by not taking things personally. People often behave without really considering the impact their actions may have on other people.

They could behave rashly without thinking about how their actions might be interpreted, or they might talk without thinking about the consequences of what they say.

We make the error of presuming someone intentionally wants to harm or offend us when we take offense at their behavior. In actuality, their actions often stem from a simple lack of self-awareness or emotional control. We can answer more clearly and impartially if we take a step back and don't take their acts personally. This prevents us from mistaking their actions as a direct assault on ourselves.

We also offer ourselves the chance to let go of our anger and resentment when we stop taking other people's behavior personally. It may be quite emotionally taxing to cling to the idea that someone has harmed us. We could obsess over what they did, mentally reliving the painful experiences, which would only make us feel worse. We release this needless emotional burden by deciding not to take their behavior personally. We give ourselves permission to go on, understanding that their actions are a reflection of their inner reality rather than our value.

We may approach future conversations with more emotional freedom and tranquility after letting go of our grudges.

Long-term, this change in viewpoint also improves our relationships. We become less reactive and more collected in our relationships with other people when we stop taking things personally. Since we no longer respond defensively or insecurely, this emotional maturity promotes better, more balanced relationships. We improve our ability to speak clearly, become more receptive, and become better listeners.Because they can express themselves honestly without worrying about inciting a defensive reaction, individuals may start to feel more at ease with us.

This makes room for more profound comprehension, more empathy, and solid bonds based on acceptance and respect for one another. In summary, developing the transforming skill of not taking other people's behavior personally may greatly enhance our mental health and interpersonal connections. We may break free from the emotional hold of fear, anger, and judgment when we acknowledge that people's actions are a mirror of their own experiences rather than of us. This enables us to approach conversations with more tolerance, empathy, and understanding, resulting in relationships that are healthier and more satisfying. We regain our emotional strength when we cease taking things personally, embracing the ability to live really and interact with others from a position of emotional maturity and self-awareness.

Discovering Power in Uncertainty and Rejection

Uncertainty and rejection are among the most difficult situations we encounter in life. They often strike out of the blue, upending our feeling of safety and value. These situations may be heartbreaking, whether they include getting turned over for a job, having a loved one reject you, or facing an unknown future. It's simple to see doubt as a sign of weakness or rejection as a personal failing.

The real power, however, lies in our capacity to interpret these events as opportunities for personal development and to find significance in them. We may achieve inner calm, resilience, and personal growth by accepting rejection and uncertainty. Any kind of rejection may be quite intimate.

We reveal our weaknesses when we put ourselves out there, whether in romantic relationships, professional endeavors, or artistic endeavors. We may start to doubt our value when we are rejected since it seems like a direct reflection of who we are. However, the reality is that rejection often has nothing to do with our own characteristics. It's a reflection of events, time, or other uncontrollable elements rather than a sign of our incompetence. We start to see that rejection is a chance for change rather than a reflection of our intrinsic value when we learn to reframe it. Even if we are unable to perceive it at the time, every rejection serves as a lesson that points us in the direction of something greater. By changing our viewpoint, we expose ourselves to new opportunities and release ourselves from the emotional weight of personalizing rejection.

Similar to rejection, uncertainty is a strong force that, depending on how we handle it, may either destroy or strengthen us. We might feel disoriented, nervous, or immobilized by the unknown during uncertain times.

It's normal to want consistency and predictability, yet these things are seldom available to us in a form that we can manage. On the other hand, accepting uncertainty offers a fantastic chance for development. It compels us to trust life's course and let go of the delusion of control. We may learn to embrace the unknown with openness and interest rather than dreading it. We may experiment with alternative strategies, pursue new avenues, and uncover hidden abilities when we are faced with uncertainty. By encouraging us to change, develop, and grow in ways that certainty just cannot, it teaches us resilience.

Our mentality holds the secret to overcoming rejection and uncertainty with strength. We have two choices when confronted with these obstacles: we either allow them to negatively define who we are, or we can take advantage of them to reinvent ourselves. In this process, having a development attitude is crucial. Rejection may be seen as a stepping stone to a greater chance rather than as the end. We may welcome uncertainty as an opportunity to develop, investigate, and create rather than seeing it as a danger.

Uncertainty and rejection are not indicators of failure; rather, they are calls to examine ourselves and find our own resilience. Every encounter offers us the chance to learn more about the world, ourselves, and our objectives.

Furthermore, uncertainty and rejection both foster emotional fortitude. When we experience rejection, we learn to deal with pain, disappointment, and anger without letting them dictate how we behave or see the world. We eventually come to understand that rejection is a brief hiccup on the road to achievement rather than a reflection of our worth. In a similar vein, uncertainty helps us maintain our composure when confronted with unclear results. We gain confidence in our capacity to handle life's uncertainties as we learn to trust both the process and ourselves. In the end, these encounters mold our emotional fortitude, giving us the strength, flexibility, and composure to meet obstacles in the future.

The feeling of liberation that comes from letting go of attachment to results is another potent component of finding strength in rejection and uncertainty. We are more prone to get frustrated when things don't go as planned when we are tied to a certain outcome, whether it is work, relationship, or objective. We have the opportunity to let go of our connection to results and instead concentrate on the here and now when faced with rejection and uncertainty. We come to believe that even in the face of uncertainty, we are headed in the right direction and that life will unfold as it is supposed to.

We may proceed with more comfort, pleasure, and serenity if we let go of the demand for control and accept life as it comes. Uncertainty and rejection can foster a greater capacity for empathy and compassion. We become more sensitive to the hardships of others when we go through these challenging emotions ourselves. Because of this insight, we are able to help, empathize, and encourage people around us who are also dealing with uncertainty or rejection. In this sense, our personal experiences turn into chances to develop closer relationships with others, encouraging mutual support and a feeling of humanity. amid addition to giving us strength, the resilience we discover amid rejection and uncertainty also improves our capacity to encourage and elevate those we come into contact with.

In the end, we must change the way we see rejection and uncertainty if we are to discover strength in them. We have the option to perceive them as stepping stones that lead us to deeper self-discovery and personal development rather than as obstacles. Rejection is an essential step on the path that leads us to something more in line with our actual purpose rather than the end of the road. Instead of being a danger, uncertainty is a catalyst for creativity and opportunity.

By accepting these difficulties with an open mind and a growth attitude, we develop the fortitude, resiliency, and clarity required to successfully negotiate life's uncertain path. In summary, rejection and uncertainty are strong accelerators for human development that should be welcomed rather than dreaded or avoided. These encounters force us to examine ourselves, reevaluate our convictions, and change the way we see success and failure.

Uncertainty gives us the strength to embrace the unknown with curiosity and confidence, while rejection teaches us to recover more resiliently. When we accept these difficulties, we are given the courage to go on because of the knowledge and lessons they provide.

When seen through the prism of personal development, rejection and uncertainty serve as stepping stones toward becoming the greatest versions of ourselves.

Using Emotional Difficulties to Create Growth Prospects

The human experience will always include emotional difficulties. Emotions may become overpowering and even paralyzing when we're coping with a terrible breakup, the death of a loved one, professional disappointments, or personal fears. These encounters have the power to completely upend us, making us doubt our capacity for coping, our value as individuals, and our role in society.But it's crucial to understand that, despite their discomfort, emotional difficulties may lead to tremendous personal development. We may turn the most trying times into valuable teachings that influence our emotional fortitude and personal development if we change the way we see things and face these obstacles with an attitude of opportunity.

Realizing that emotions, despite their intensity, are not always bad is the first step in transforming emotional difficulties into learning experiences.
Emotions are only indicators that something in our life needs our attention. Sadness, anger, fear, and anxiety are all natural human emotions that often reveal more profound truths about who we are and the world around us.

We make room for recovery and development when we start to embrace and recognize our feelings instead of denying or repressing them. Emotions may be seen as opportunities to examine our inner selves, pinpoint areas in which we might be having difficulty, and take proactive measures toward good transformation rather than as barriers. This change in viewpoint enables us to welcome emotional difficulties as a chance for personal growth and development. Developing emotional awareness is one of the most important strategies for transforming emotional difficulties into chances for personal development. It's simple to respond impulsively to intense emotions by becoming angry, withdrawing, or avoiding situations.

However, we may learn more about the underlying reasons of our emotions by engaging in mindfulness exercises and increasing our awareness of our emotional triggers.

We may start to regulate our responses rather than letting emotions rule us. We may overcome habitual behavioral patterns and react to difficulties with more clarity, discernment, and purpose when we possess this emotional awareness. We may start to identify the fundamental problems at work and open the door to healing and development by comprehending the underlying causes of our emotions.

Developing emotional resilience is another effective strategy for transforming emotional difficulties into chances for development. The capacity to overcome adversity, adjust to change, and go on despite difficulties is resilience. Developing emotional resilience is learning to deal with challenging emotions with poise and power rather than ignoring or numbing them. Reframing difficulties as chances for development rather than threats is one strategy to increase resilience. We might ask ourselves, "What can I learn from this?" when we encounter hardship. How can this make me stronger? We give ourselves the ability to use every emotional setback as a springboard for increased emotional maturity and personal growth when we reframe our difficulties in this manner.

The practice of self-compassion is another essential component in transforming emotional difficulties into chances for personal development. It's simple to be harsh with ourselves when we're experiencing challenging feelings. We can think we're not handling things well enough, that we're weak, or that we're failing. Self-criticism, however, just makes the agony worse and prolongs our suffering.

Rather, we might treat ourselves with the same consideration and understanding that we would provide to a close friend in a comparable circumstance by engaging in self-compassion exercises. Self-compassion entails accepting our emotional suffering without passing judgment, letting ourselves experience it without feeling guilty, and taking action to take good care of ourselves. This self-acceptance and self-love practice builds resilience and long-term development while also promoting emotional healing.

Additionally, emotional difficulties provide a chance to develop closer relationships with other people. We might be inclined to withdraw when we are experiencing painful emotions, either because we are ashamed of being vulnerable or because we are afraid of burdening other people. But talking to a therapist, family member, or trusted friend about our emotional difficulties may be a very effective method to develop and heal. By being vulnerable, we enable people to connect with us and provide support, insight, and understanding. We often get fresh perspectives and knowledge from these relationships, which may improve our ability to deal with emotional difficulties.

Sharing our difficulties also serves as a reminder that we are not alone and that others have similar emotional challenges. By working together, we can help one another on our path to recovery and development. It's important to keep in mind that our emotions do not determine who we are when we encounter emotional difficulties. Emotions are a normal aspect of life, but they don't define who we are as people. We recover control over our emotional state when we acknowledge that we have the ability to decide how we react to our feelings. We can face emotional difficulties with more bravery and confidence when we feel empowered. We may recognize our feelings, sit with them, and then deliberately choose how we want to go rather than letting them control us. One of the characteristics of emotional development and maturity is the capacity to choose our own reactions as opposed to letting our feelings dictate them.

Additionally, emotional difficulties can provide a chance to reevaluate our objectives and ideals. It's normal to consider our priorities while we are experiencing challenging emotions. These difficulties may operate as a wake-up call, encouraging us to reorient our decisions and behaviors in accordance with our basic beliefs. For instance, losing our job or having a difficult relationship might make us reevaluate what it is that makes us happy or fulfilled.

This introspective process enables us to reassess our life's trajectory and make necessary corrections, resulting in a more genuine and meaningful existence. Lastly, emotional difficulties allow us to learn to be patient with ourselves.

It's crucial to accept ourselves while we work through emotional challenges since healing and development are not quick fixes. Emotional wounds need time, introspection, and attention to heal, just as physical ones do. Being patient with ourselves and realizing that development happens gradually helps us become more resilient and self-compassionate. Every emotional obstacle serves as a chance to exercise patience, respect our emotional path, and have faith that we will eventually come out stronger and more complete.

In summary, emotional difficulties are chances for development and change rather than something to be feared or avoided. We might transform suffering into meaning by reinterpreting these events as opportunities for introspection, emotional fortitude, and closer relationships with others. We may overcome our emotional obstacles with grace, courage, and wisdom if we have self-compassion, emotional awareness, and patience. When we accept that every emotional difficulty is an opportunity for development, we start to see these experiences as opportunities to become the finest, most genuine versions of ourselves rather than as setbacks.

CONCLUSION: ACCEPTING THEM AS A LIFESTYLE

As our exploration of the "Let Them" hypothesis draws to a close, it is evident that this simple but strong idea has the capacity to revolutionize every facet of our lives. Adopting the "Let Them" lifestyle involves more than simply allowing others to live their lives as they see fit; it also entails realizing that contentment, progress, and serenity arise from relinquishing control and having faith in life's natural course. We liberate ourselves from needless stress and expectations when we take a backseat and let others be who they really are, make their own choices, and travel their own paths. Additionally, we build a society in which people are empowered to be who they really are, appreciated, and supported.

The foundation of this way of life is the understanding that every individual is on a unique route, and no two journeys are the same. It's about realizing that, while we may help and encourage others, we cannot and should not control how others live.It becomes simpler to accept that other people may make decisions that we may not understand or agree with the more we adopt this approach.

We may take a backseat, support them when necessary, and have faith in their capacity to make choices that are in their best interests rather than imposing our own agenda. By doing this, we discover that we are more content with life's organic flow and the variety of experiences it offers. For ourselves as well as for others, relinquishing control is a liberating experience. We let life develop in its own time and rhythm when we let go of the impulse to control every result. We are encouraged to become more thoughtful, empathetic, and present throughout this process. It tells us that we may live more joyfully and with less resistance if we have faith in both ourselves and other people.

This feeling of independence is very freeing; it enables us to prioritize our own development and contentment while honoring the development and contentment of others around us. We make room for love, empathy, and connection to flourish when we let go of our urge to control and correct. The effect that adopting a "Let Them" lifestyle has on our relationships is among its most significant features. We encourage people to be authentic rather than pressuring them to live up to our standards. This fosters an atmosphere of acceptance and respect where each person may develop at their own rate.

Letting individuals be who they are builds a strong feeling of trust and understanding, whether in friendships, love relationships, or family dynamics. We become encouraging partners on their path, just as they are on ours, and we no longer feel the need to shape or alter other people.

Adopting "Let Them" improves not just our connections with other people but also our relationships with ourselves. It pushes us to stop criticizing ourselves and striving for perfection. We start living genuinely when we learn to accept ourselves with all of our imperfections and stop looking for acceptance. Because of this authenticity, we are able to make choices that are in line with our own wants rather than what other people believe is best for us. We grow more certain of our decisions, less preoccupied with criticism from others, and more in line with our inner truth when we accept our individuality.

This in turn produces an inner feeling of contentment and serenity that is impervious to other people's thoughts or deeds. Adopting the "Let Them" way of life also means accepting flaws in other people and ourselves. Life is chaotic, uncertain, and fraught with difficulties. We get increasingly worn out and irritated the more we attempt to control or influence events.

We enable ourselves and others to make errors, grow from them, and learn from them when we embrace this attitude. This flaw is what gives existence its depth and significance. We discover our actual strength and resilience when we face difficulties, overcome barriers, and suffer failures. For the benefit of others as well as ourselves, the "Let Them" concept exhorts us to accept this flawed process.

We also start to see that respect is fundamental when we allow others to live their lives as they see fit. Allowing someone to pursue their own path, even if it deviates from our own, is a basic manifestation of love. A foundation of mutual respect and trust is established when one respects another's independence, decisions, and path without passing judgment. We understand that genuine relationships are based on support and freedom rather than dominance or manipulation. We not only help others succeed when we allow them to flourish in their own manner, but we also improve our own lives by fostering closer relationships and more common experiences.

Adopting "Let Them" promotes an inclusive, understanding, and empathetic culture in society at large. Given that every individual's experience adds to the overall fabric of existence, it inspires us to acknowledge and value variety. Allowing others to live freely makes it possible for individuals to be who they really are without worrying about criticism or rejection.

As a result, more individuals are inspired to accept who they really are and make constructive contributions to the world. Allowing individuals to be themselves contributes to a society that is more understanding, caring, and peaceful.

In the end, "Let Them" is a way of living rather than just a theory or philosophy. It's a philosophy that calls for patience, an open heart, and everyday practice.

We make room for love, acceptance, and development when we choose this lifestyle and let go of the impulse to dominate, correct, or condemn. Our interactions with others and, more significantly, with ourselves are changed by this simple but powerful exercise. One moment at a time, we discover how to appreciate the beauty of life as it presents itself, trust, and let go. To sum up, adopting a "Let Them" lifestyle encourages us to live a happier, more peaceful, and more fulfilled existence.

It enables us to enjoy the individual experiences of others, let go of the urge for control, and have faith in life's process. In addition to improving our relationships and personal development, adopting this attitude makes the world a more sympathetic and understanding place.
Letting go is a show of strength, bravery, and wisdom rather than weakness.

We enable ourselves and others to thrive when we adopt the "Let Them" mindset, which releases us from the limitations of judgment and control and opens us up to the richness of life.

The Liberation Acquired Through Letting Go

We often feel ourselves bound by responsibilities, expectations, and the overpowering drive to control results in life. This need for control may become oppressive, whether it is over our relationships, our professional trajectories, or even the most trivial aspects of day-to-day existence. What if letting go, rather than gaining greater control, is the secret to real freedom? Letting go offers a tremendous and revolutionary freedom that leads to a life of real pleasure, clarity, and calm.

We allow ourselves to experience the fullness of life in its purest form when we let go of the impulse to control every part of our lives. Letting go entails trusting life's process and letting go of our hold on results, not giving up. Everybody has a propensity to have certain expectations for how things should go, depending on their ideals or vision. But life often goes in a different direction than we anticipate, and it is at those times of surrender that we find a greater feeling of freedom. Instead of always aiming for an ideal that could or might not come true, the concept of letting go is based on acceptance—not apathy, but on allowing ourselves to be present with what is occurring in the moment. It is letting go of attachment to certain results and accepting life as it comes, understanding that every experience—even the challenging ones—has something worthwhile to contribute.

Giving up control over other people's decisions is one of the biggest sources of freedom. Believing that our way is the best for someone we care about, whether it be a friend, lover, or even a kid, we often attempt to guide their life. But real freedom arises when we let others make their own choices, even if we disagree with them. We respect their autonomy and make room for them to develop and flourish in their own manner by letting go of the need to correct, guide, or control their pathways.

This not only frees them, but it also frees us from the weight of attempting to dictate every element of another person's existence. This letting go gives us a great deal of freedom, enabling us to concentrate on our own development and contentment free from the burden of other people's decisions.The freedom it offers in terms of inner calm is another potent feature of letting go. When things don't go as planned, we often feel nervous, dissatisfied, or upset because we are tied to certain results or expectations.

These emotions are a consequence of our need to exert control, forecast, and ensure a certain outcome. We can, however, accept whatever comes our way more easily after we let go of these attachments.

Accepting that we have no control over anything is more important than deciding to live a passive life. This mental change produces a deep sensation of serenity. We learn to flow with the river rather than resist it all the time, adjusting to the whims and turns life presents. We are able to live life more completely and genuinely when we are free from worry and disappointment.

Emotional release is another sort of liberation that comes with letting go. When we harbor grudges, unsolved difficulties, or prior wounds, we are burdened with needless emotional baggage.

We may break free from the grip that these previous events have on our life by letting go of them without discounting or disregarding them. We cease allowing past traumas to dictate our present and future. We may recover and go on without being constrained by the past thanks to this emotional release. We recover our emotional energy and channel it toward more constructive endeavors when we let go of the hurt, bitterness, and rage that may have previously imprisoned us. Because it allows us to develop and achieve pleasure without being continuously drawn back into old suffering, the freedom that results from this emotional release is a gift.

Letting go may also result in deeper, more lasting ties in relationships. We often go into partnerships with the implicit assumption that the other person will act in a certain manner, satisfy our demands, or conform to the stereotype we have of them. We lose the chance to really connect with the person as they are when we cling to these preconceived notions. An atmosphere of sincere connection and understanding is produced by letting go of these preconceptions and enabling people to appear as who they really are. It permits respect for one another, allowing everyone to be themselves without feeling compelled to live up to artificial standards.

Deeper ties and stronger relationships are fostered by this freedom, where love and support are freely given without the need to manipulate or alter one another.

Additionally, letting go results in a feeling of empowerment. We regain our power when we quit attempting to exert control over every circumstance.
We come to see that our capacity to handle life with grace and resiliency, rather than controlling every aspect of it, is what really makes us strong. Giving up control allows us to believe in our own ability to adapt and flourish rather than feeling the need to constantly push things into place. This change of viewpoint gives us the ability to take charge of our life in a manner that feels genuine and satisfying. We learn to face life with confidence and inner strength rather than feeling overburdened by outside forces. Enjoying the present moment is another aspect of the freedom that comes with letting go. We often get mired in regrets about the past or anxieties about the future, which keeps us from living in the now. We allow ourselves to appreciate the beauty of the here and now when we let go of the drive to control. We value what is occurring in our life at the moment and stop waiting for the ideal moment, the ideal situation, or the ideal result.

We can enjoy life's little pleasures and recognize the depth of every experience because this attentiveness provides us serenity and satisfaction.

Last but not least, relinquishing control opens the door to potential new experiences and chances. We can be shutting ourselves up to alternative options when we adhere to a certain strategy or goal.

Living a Life of Harmony, Development, and Genuine Joy

It's simple to get engrossed in the hustle of attempting to fulfill obligations, achieve success, and meet expectations in our fast-paced environment. There is often little space for tranquility, personal development, or true pleasure amid the never-ending struggle. However, we may live a life that is not only tranquil but also full of personal growth and profound, enduring enjoyment by adopting an attitude that promotes letting go. A change in perspective is necessary to live a life of serenity, development, and genuine pleasure; we must stop looking for satisfaction in material accomplishments and begin nurturing it within. Letting rid of the impulse to exert control over our surroundings is the first step toward achieving serenity.

We are often taught that when we have everything under control—including our relationships, professions, and even our emotional reactions—peace will arrive. But when we let go of this incessant drive to control and micromanage every part of our life, genuine serenity emerges. We may escape the never-ending cycle of worry and annoyance that results from trying to control things that are often beyond our control when we learn to accept life as it is.

The calm that results from letting go is not about being passive; rather, it is about embracing life as it comes, having faith in our ability to deal with any challenges, and living in the present without worrying about how things should proceed. Letting go naturally leads to spiritual and psychological growth. We make room for fresh experiences and opportunities when we let go of our connection to expectations. We let go of antiquated ideas, habits, and anxieties that restrict our potential. Rather, we make room for fresh viewpoints, ideas, and chances to enter our life. When we give ourselves permission to attempt new things, go outside of our comfort zones, and take lessons from every experience—good or bad—we grow. We make space for change when we let go of the past, including previous relationships, past errors, and past wounds.

Growth occurs when we embrace the present with curiosity and openness rather than being constrained by things that no longer serve us. Living really and accepting life's path is the path to true pleasure, the type that isn't reliant on outside factors. Genuine pleasure may arise when we release ourselves from peer pressure, comparison, and the need for perfection. Appreciating the little things, like the comfort of being with loved ones, the beauty of nature, the warmth of a hug, or the accomplishment of a personal goal, is the source of true pleasure. We feel the most delight when we are totally present and not preoccupied with finding anything "better" or "more." We may embrace our value from inside and find satisfaction in who we are rather than what we own or achieve when we let go of external affirmation. When we stop looking for joy outside of ourselves and acknowledge that it already exists inside us, waiting to be felt at every single instant, joy pours.

It is not about arriving at a place to live a life of tranquility, development, and happiness. It involves making the consistent decision to let go of things that no longer serve us and accepting each stage of the process with appreciation, openness, and faith. It's about embracing the beauty of imperfection and letting go of the expectations that come with striving for perfection.

When we stop battling life's obstacles and begin overcoming them with fortitude, peace results.

When we accept every event as a chance to learn and overcome our fear of failing, we may grow. When we learn to find satisfaction in the simple act of being totally present in life, rather than in material possessions or accomplishments, we may create true joy. Living a life that feels in line with your own self is what it means to be peaceful, happy, and growing. It's about accepting yourself as you are, having faith in your own path, and letting your inner serenity, curiosity, and thankfulness lead the way.

The ability to fully experience life in all its complexity and richness is made possible when we let go of the things that keep us back, such as our need for control, our fear of failing, and our need for approval. The end result is a life that is full of serenity, development, and genuine pleasure rather than one that is just about getting by or surviving.By living this manner, we demonstrate to the world that inner serenity comes from inside rather than from worldly possessions or approval from others.

Growth is about accepting the process of self-discovery and learning, not about aiming for perfection. And the freedom of letting go, the contentment that comes from understanding that we are sufficient just the way we are, and the present are where genuine pleasure may be discovered. We are intended to live this life—one that is filled with pleasure, progress, and tranquility. It is a way of being that we may develop daily rather than a goal to be attained.

Made in the USA
Monee, IL
07 January 2025

76315815R00059